He Spoke From The Cross

Larry A. Brookins

HE SPOKE FROM THE CROSS

Copyright © 2016 Larry A. Brookins for LA Brookins Ministries

ISBN: 978-1-939654-7-48

All rights reserved solely by the author under International Copyright Law. No part of this book may be reproduced in any form stored in a retrieval system, or transmitted by any means without written permission from the author, Larry A. Brookins. Except where designated, the author certifies that all contents are original and do not infringe upon the legal rights of any other person or work.

All Scripture quotations, unless otherwise indicated are taken from the New King James Version®. Copyright © 1982 by Thomas Nelson. Used by permission. All rights reserved. Scripture identified NIV® are taken from the New International Version®, Copyright © 1973, 1978, 1984, 2011 by Biblica, Inc.® Used by permission. All rights reserved worldwide. Scripture identified NLT are taken from New Living Translation copyright© 1996, 2004, 2007, 2013 by Tyndale House Foundation. Used by permission of Tyndale House Publishers Inc., Carol Stream, Illinois 60188. All rights reserved. Scripture identified AMP are taken from the Amplified® Bible, Copyright © 1954, 1958, 1962, 1964, 1965, 1987 by The Lockman Foundation. Used by permission. (www.Lockman.org) Scripture identified NCV are taken from the New Century Version®. Copyright © 2005 by Thomas Nelson. Used by permission. All rights reserved.

Editor: Charlotte Brookins-Hudson, Esq.

Cover Image: Unknown Source

Cover Design: Chiquita George

Back Cover Photo: Renee K. Robinson

Title Page Image: Courtesy of 4.bp.blogspot.com

Printed in the United States

10 9 8 7 6 5 4 3 2 1

Published by: Life to Legacy, LLC

877-267-7477

Life2Legacy.com

Dedication

I dedicate this book project to all of the men and women of God who have not strayed away from the preaching of the cross. The Apostle Paul says, "For the preaching of the cross is to them that perish foolishness; but unto us which are saved it is the power of God" (1 Corinthians 1:18, KJV). There is no way we can, or should underestimate the significance and impact of what occurred at Calvary some 2,000 plus years ago. It was here that God displayed His great love for all of mankind (John 3:16; Romans 5:8); a love that opened up the door to salvation and redemption for "whosoever will" (Revelation 22:17), and a love that enables us to enjoy the forgiveness of sin and the renewal of divine fellowship. I say to my fellow clergymen and women: "Keep preaching the cross. Keep telling the story. Keep pointing others to the place where Satan and sin were defeated and where victory was achieved for us simply because Jesus willingly laid down His life for us." "But He was wounded for our transgressions, He was bruised for our iniquities; the chastisement for our peace was upon Him, and by His stripes we are healed" (Isaiah 53:5). I declare, as did the Apostle Paul: "But God forbid that I should boast except in the cross of our Lord Jesus Christ, by whom the world has been crucified to me, and I to the world" (Galatians 6:14).

"And when they had come to the place called Calvary, there they crucified Him, and the criminals, one on the right hand and the other on the left. Then Jesus said . . . ."

Luke 23:33-34(a)

Table Of Contents

And being found in fashion as a man, he humbled himself, and became obedient unto death, even the death of the cross.
Philippians 2:8 (KJV)

Foreword

I am humbled to have been asked to provide this Foreword to *He Spoke from the Cross.* While I am a lawyer and not a theologian or minister by training, I firmly believe in applying the Apostle Paul's words in Second Timothy 2:15: "*Be diligent to present yourself approved to God, a worker who does not need to be ashamed, rightly dividing the word of truth.*" I should note at the outset that the author is not only my brother in Christ, but he is also my biological brother. Rev. Dr. Larry A. Brookins serves as the senior pastor of the True Foundation Transformation Church, which is located in Chicago, Illinois. True Foundation is my "home church" where I was baptized, received my spiritual foundation, and attended until I relocated to Washington, D.C.

Over the years I have followed my brother's growth in the ministry, read all the books he has authored, as well as many of his manuscripts, and I am proud to say that I am one of his biggest supporters. My support is not primarily based on our familial relationship, but I support my brother's work in the ministry because he has a strong gift of preaching, teaching, and writing. As is evidenced by his extensive body of written work, he is enthusiastically and sincerely interested in empowering others to study to show themselves workers who need not be ashamed by equipping them to "rightly divide the word of truth." What my brother writes he preaches, what my brother preaches he teaches, and what my brother teaches he lives.

In this, his latest book, the author methodically walks us through the seven words spoken by Jesus as He endured the most blatantly unjust act of injustice. The book's setting is at the cross where

God is at His best and man is at his worst. During the 2016 Lent Season, Rev. Dr. Brookins preached what has become the groundwork for this book. From the seven sermons he preached he extrapolates seven lessons applicable to all humanity. Seven is the number of completion and perfection. Seven days were involved in creation. There are seven days of the week and the Sabbath is on the seventh day. Rev. Dr. Brookins has written about the seven churches in the Book of Revelation (*Seven Things that God Hates & Seven Letters to Seven Churches*, AuthorHouse 2010).

He Spoke from the Cross is a transformative book which is a must have for any biblical scholar's library and it will serve as a helpful reference and resource tool. This book contains words that will equip believers to minister in their homes, community, churches, and throughout the world. Rev. Dr. Brookins uses the words Jesus spoke from the cross to show us how the unforgivable can be forgiven, how to show compassion even while dealing with painful moments in our life, to remind us to take care of our family responsibilities, what to do when our prayers are not answered in the way we want them answered, how to respond when we feel forgotten or forsaken, and in many other ways to show us the eternal value in choosing a purpose filled life. Even if the lessons do not currently apply to you, just keep living. In the words of Dr. H. Beecher Hicks, Jr., you are "either coming out of a storm, in a storm, or heading for a storm" (*Preaching Through a Storm*, Zondervan 1987).

The lessons in this book will teach you how to persevere during the darkest and most painfully agonizing times and it will encourage you to give God the glory in the midst of it all. In spite of what you might be going through, this book teaches us to be strong and courageous. It teaches us how to trust God. It teaches us how to remain faithful to God. It teaches us how to depend on God. It teaches us, no matter what life brings our way, to always put our lives in God's hands and to keep them there. I know that this book will bless your life. I know that this book will edify your soul. I know that this book will stimulate your thoughts. I know that this book will uplift your spirit. Jesus spoke from the cross. May we be attentive to what He said and to what His words are still declaring to us.

Charlotte Brookins-Hudson, Esquire

Introduction

Looking down from the cross seven times Jesus spoke. In each spoken word there is a message and a lesson. In each spoken word we glimpse the humanity of Jesus, or the heart of Jesus, or the mission of Jesus, or the compassion that Jesus still had for others even while He was dying on a cross. As he hung for six excruciating hours suffering for our sins and being wounded, bruised, and battered in order to provide for us the opportunity of being redeemed from the penalty of sin, which is *death*, and reconciled to God, which is *life*; seven times Jesus opened His mouth fulfilling prophecy and revealing, through His words, who He really was (and still is) and what He came to earth to do. But for these seven expressions, Jesus remained relatively silent and in extreme agony as He observed, listened, and contemplated while nailed to a cross.

Had you stood in the crowd that day watching Jesus die, you would have heard Him utter seven astounding statements that grants us the privilege of peering into the mind of Jesus during the very time that He was accomplishing the will of His Father as the "Lamb slain from the foundation of the world" (Revelation 13:8). You would have heard Him say: "Father, forgive them, for they do not know what they do" (Luke 23:33). You would have heard Him say: "Assuredly, I say to you, today you will be with Me in Paradise" (Luke 23:43). You would have heard Him say: "Woman, behold your son" (John 19:26) and "Behold your mother" (John 19:27)! You would have heard Him say: "Eli, Eli, lama sabachthani," interpreted: "My God, My God, why have You forsaken Me" (Matthew 27:46)? You would have heard Him say: "I thirst" (John 19:28)! You would have heard Him say: "It is finished" (John 19:30)! And then finally, before Jesus bows His head and breathes His last breath, you would have heard Him say: "Father, 'into Your hands I commit My spirit'" (Luke 23:46). It starts with "Father." It ends with "Father." But so much is embedded in every word that Jesus spoke.

This book is a byproduct of the privilege I had of expounding each word, as I preached on each during the course of seven weeks at True Foundation Transformation Church (Chicago), where I serve as Senior Pastor. The chapters in this book are not sermon manuscripts, but the divine inspiration of God as communicated to me for revelation, edification, information, and instruction. It is my prayer that what is written in the pages of this book will enlighten you as to why Jesus said what He said and what relevance His words are intended to have to us today. Although we were not at the cross of Calvary physically, through the records of Scripture, we are. We are there with so many who are gathered around the cross for various reasons. So while we are there, let us listen and learn. Let us draw near the cross as our Savior hangs, bleeding from the crown of thorns that was placed on His head, and bleeding from the nails that were thrust into both of His hands and feet. Let us not forget the many lashes He painfully endured on His back for us. Yet, fatigued and nearing death, Jesus had something to say. Let us eavesdrop via the writings of the Gospel writers of Matthew, Luke, and John to Jesus as: HE SPOKE FROM THE CROSS.

Rev. Dr. Larry A. Brookins
President/CEO
LA Brookins Ministries, Inc.
www.labrookinsministries.org
Senior Pastor
True Foundation Transformation Church
Chicago, IL
www.tftchurch.org

"And when they had come to the place called Calvary, there they crucified Him, and the criminals, one on the right hand and the other on the left. Then Jesus said, 'FATHER, FORGIVE THEM, FOR THEY DO NOT KNOW WHAT THEY DO.'"

Luke 23:33-34

Chapter One

Father, Forgive Them

(Theme: FORGIVENESS)

It is only befitting that the very first words that Jesus utters from the cross are words of forgiveness. It only makes sense because the point of the cross is forgiveness. It only makes sense because Jesus is on the cross so sins could be forgiven. It only makes sense because His blood is shed for forgiveness. It only makes sense because His body is broken for forgiveness. It only makes sense because His life is rendered for forgiveness. It only makes sense because His reason for coming was to offer Himself as a mediator or facilitator of forgiveness. It only makes sense because the people who crucified Him needed forgiveness. It only makes sense because those gathered around Him at the cross needed forgiveness. It only makes sense because the thieves who hung next to Him needed forgiveness. More importantly, it only makes sense because you and I are in constant need of forgiveness. We need what Jesus came to do. We need what Jesus did on the cross. We need what Jesus said from the cross, "Father, forgive them" (Luke 23:34).

From the cross Jesus practices what He preached. During the course of His ministry He taught us to forgive: to forgive those who trespass against us (Matthew 6:12), to love our enemies and to do good to those who hate us (Matthew 5:44), to forgive without limit (Matthew 18:21-22) and to forgive without discrimination (Luke 17:3-4). From the cross Jesus exemplifies or demonstrates what is expected of us in our skirmishes with other people; though people lie on us, we should say: Father, forgive them; though people talk about us, we should say: Father, forgive them; though people criticize us, we should say: Father, forgive them; though people oppose us and persecute us, we should say: Father, forgive them; though people abandon us: Father, forgive them; though people mishandle us: Father, forgive them; though people reject us: Father, forgive them; though people shame us and sometimes defame us: Father, forgive them. In forgiving others, we take on the spirit of Christ and that of the cross. In forgiving others, we exhibit and transmit the will of God. The will of God is that we forgive others even as He, for the sake of Christ, forgives us (Ephesians 4:32). Forgiveness puts us in harmony with God and forgiveness makes us true representatives of God. While hanging on a cross Jesus, looking out and looking around says, "Father, forgive them, for they do not know what they do" (Luke 23:34).

The individuals who crucified Jesus were not aware of the full scope of what they were doing because they did not really know who Jesus was. In essence, these were ignorant of the identity of Jesus and unmindful of His divinity. Being blinded by hatred and manipulated by Satan, they did not realize that the One of whom they were executing was the One responsible for their existence that in Jesus is salvation and through Jesus is life everlasting—that in Jesus is regeneration and transformation and through Jesus is justification and glorification—that the Messiah they longed for now hung before them on a cross. To this those who crucified Jesus were ignorant, but ignorance is not an excuse, nor does ignorance exonerate their actions, or ours. Their actions were deplorable. Their actions were despicable. But in spite of their actions Jesus says, "Father, forgive them." They did not deserve forgiveness but still He says, "Father, forgive them." Still it is: 'Father, pardon them.' Still it is: 'Father, release them.' Still it is: 'Father, make an allowance for them.' Still it is: 'Father, acquit them of their guilt.' Do not punish them. Do not condemn them. Do not blame them. Put their indiscretions on my account.

In the midst of being mocked; in the midst of being spat upon; in the midst of being whipped, slapped, and having hair plucked from His beard Jesus says, "Father, forgive them." In the midst of being depleted of human strength, and depleted of human blood, and depleted of human dignity, and stripped of His clothing, as well as nailed to a cross, still Jesus says, "Father, forgive them." Jesus was even betrayed by one of His own disciples (Judas Iscariot). Jesus was even denied three times by one of His own disciples (Peter). All of Jesus' disciples abandoned Him when the Roman soldiers arrested Him, but still the first word is: "Father, forgive them, for they do not know what they do" (Luke 23:34). In this Jesus prays an intercessory prayer. An intercessory prayer is "an entreaty in favor of another." It is a prayer or petition to God on behalf of someone else. When Jesus said, "Father, forgive them," He was making an appeal for divine grace, not for Himself, but for everyone who played a part in getting Jesus to the cross and having Jesus crucified on the cross; and even for Judas, who betrayed Him and Peter, who denied Him, and for all of His disciples, who fled for their lives in fear. What is the relevancy of what Jesus said *then* for us *now*?

The relevancy is: forgiveness is still available. The relevancy is: no matter the crime or the sin, past, present, or future, at the cross of Jesus mercy awaits and pardon is possible. The relevancy is: there is a promise in God's Word of transformation and absolution. Hear the words of Isaiah 1:18, "Come now, let us settle the matter," says the LORD. "Though your sins are like scarlet, they shall be as white as snow; though they are red as crimson, they shall be like wool" (NIV). Jesus came here and gave His life to make forgiveness, not only available, but obtainable. The relevancy is: there is forgiveness in Christ. The relevancy is:

there is forgiveness before the Throne of God's grace. Because of Jesus, forgiveness is in your reach. Because of Jesus, forgiveness is now an option. I speak to someone who is having difficulty believing that God will forgive you. I speak to someone who cannot quite forgive yourself. You messed up, but the truth is; we all do! The truth is: "All have sinned and fall short of the glory of God" (Romans 3:23). The truth is: "There is none righteous, no, not one" (Romans 3:10). I speak to someone in your struggle to forgive somebody else. The relevancy is: forgiveness is the way if we desire or expect to be forgiven by God. Hear what Jesus says in Matthew 6:14-15 (NLT):

"If you forgive those who sin against you, your Heavenly Father will forgive you. But if you refuse to forgive others, your Father will not forgive your sins."

The message is clear. There can be no healing without forgiveness. The message is clear. There can be no recovery without forgiveness. The message is clear. There can be no resolution without forgiveness. The message is clear. There can be no reconciliation without forgiveness. Forgiveness cleanses. Forgiveness makes us whole. Forgiveness unites. Forgiveness reunites. In forgiveness, God chooses to wipe away our sins. In forgiveness, God allows us to come home again. In forgiveness, God destroys all evidence against us. In forgiveness, God extends to us another chance; another chance to live again; another chance to love again; another chance to laugh again; another chance to enjoy divine fellowship and relationship. It is another chance to regain what was taken. It is another chance to find what was lost. It is another chance to build up what was torn down. It is another chance to embrace again what sin stripped away.

This is the beauty of forgiveness. This is the power of the cross. It is written in Scripture: "Without shedding of blood there is no remission" (Hebrews 9:22). Remission is "the cancellation of a debt, charge, or penalty." Remission is "the relinquishment of a payment, obligation, etc." This is what happened at Calvary. This is what Jesus did for us at Calvary. At Calvary, our debt was negated. At Calvary, our sin charge was dropped. At Calvary, the penalty of sin (death) was paid in full. At Calvary, forgiveness was made possible because Jesus died for us. Because Jesus died, we are free. Because Jesus died, we are justified. Because Jesus died, we have been reconnected to God. Because Jesus said, "Father, forgive them," the Father has forgiven us. I have been forgiven, and if your faith is in Jesus, you too have been forgiven. I have been made whole, and if your faith is in Jesus, you too have been made whole. My life is new, and if your faith is in Jesus, your life too is new. My name is written in God's Book of redemption, and if your faith is in Jesus, your name is there too! The message and the lesson in Jesus' first words from the cross is FORGIVENESS.

Jesus said it on our behalf, now it is time for you and I to say it on behalf of someone else: Father, forgive them. Father, forgive my haters. Father, forgive my enemies. Father, forgive my adversaries. Father, forgive those who speak ill of me. Father, forgive those who mistreat me. Father, forgive those who neglect me. Father, forgive those who desert me. Father, forgive those who hurt me. Jesus did it for us, why not *us* do it for others? Why not intercede for others? Why not mediate for others? Why not plead for others? Why not ask God to do for others what Jesus asked God to do for us? Why not say, "Father, forgive them?" Some people may know what they do to us and some may not; however, knowledge is not the issue; the issue is forgiveness. Forgiveness is God's way. Forgiveness is Jesus' way. Forgiveness is the way and the word of the cross. So the next time you are lied on say what Jesus said, "Father, forgive them." So the next time you are mistreated say what Jesus said, "Father, forgive them." So the next time people walk out of your life say what Jesus said, "Father, forgive them." So the next time people hurt you, on purpose or by accident, say what Jesus said, "Father, forgive them." Take your antagonists to the cross. Take every backstabber to the cross. Take every troublemaker to the cross. Take the crucifiers of your life to the cross. Take them to the cross and there say what Jesus said, "Father, forgive them." Let go of whatever is done or said that brings discomfort to you. Release it. Expunge it. Liberate yourself by forgiving it. Forgive it and forgive them, say what Jesus said, "FATHER, FORGIVE THEM, FOR THEY DO NOT KNOW WHAT THEY DO." Now let us turn our attention to what Jesus says next.

"Then one of the criminals who were hanged blasphemed Him, saying, 'If You are the Christ, save Yourself and us.' But the other, answering, rebuked him, saying, 'Do you not even fear God, seeing you are under the same condemnation? And we indeed justly, for we receive the due reward of our deeds; but this Man has done nothing wrong.' Then he said to Jesus, 'Lord, remember me when You come into Your Kingdom.' And Jesus said to him, 'ASSUREDLY, I SAY TO YOU, TODAY YOU WILL BE WITH ME IN PARADISE.'"

Luke 23:39-43

Chapter Two

Today,

You Will Be With Me In Paradise

(Theme: SALVATION)

As we continue examining the words of Jesus as spoken from the cross we return again to Calvary, the place where Jesus was crucified as a propitiation for our sins (1 John 2:2). The term *propitiation* projects the thought of Jesus incurring the wrath of God as proxy for us. *Proxy* means that He stood or hung as a substitute for us. This conveys the fact that what Jesus did, He did in order to secure for us the mercy of God and God's grace in place of us receiving punishment from God for our transgressions against God. Without a doubt, from the fall of Adam in the Garden of Eden until now, and even beyond now until the Second Coming of Christ, all of mankind, inclusive of you and I, have violated, and will continue to violate the commandments of God for which we are entitled to death. The Bible states clearly in Romans 6:23 that "the wages of sin is death." Because the wages of sin is death, somebody had to pay the price required of sin. Thus, because He loves us (John 3:16; Romans 5:8), God took it upon Himself to offer His Son Jesus on behalf of us because the price required of sin was far too much for us to pay.

What Jesus endured for us, before the cross and while on the cross, we could not endure for ourselves. How Jesus suffered for us, before the cross and while on the cross, no one but Jesus would consent to do. With foreknowledge of the pain and of the sorrow surrounding the cross and with the premonition of the agony and persecution leading up to and including the cross, Jesus relinquished His will in preference for and in deference to His Father's will. It was His Father's will that He die on the cross for our sins. Isaiah 53:10 declares, "It pleased the LORD to bruise Him." So on the cross we encounter Jesus and from the cross we hear Jesus speak seven times from "Father, forgive them, for they do not know what they do" (Luke 23:34) to "Father, into Your hands I commit My spirit" (Luke 23:46).

In Luke 23:46 we hear Jesus speaking for the second time to one of the malefactors who hung alongside of Him. A *malefactor* is a criminal, a convicted felon, a hoodlum, a lawbreaker, a thug. On both sides of Jesus were individuals who were guilty of the crimes they were crucified for. In the accounts of the crucifixion of Jesus recorded in the Gospels of Matthew and Mark (Matthew 27:38; Mark 15:27), these two individuals are referred to as "thieves." In the prophecy of Isaiah 53:12 they are called "transgressors."

> "He was numbered with the transgressors, and He bore the sin of many, and made intercession for the transgressors."

On Calvary, Jesus hangs between these two sinful men as the Just for the unjust, or as the Righteous One for all who could have hung, justifiably, on either the left side of Jesus or on His right. Those qualified to hang next to Jesus includes you and I. Jesus was dying on a cross for us.

The life of Jesus was a mission of love. The life of Jesus was a mission of sacrifice, and His death was no exception: "For God so loved the world that He gave His only begotten Son, that whoever believes in Him should not perish but have everlasting life" (John 3:16). God loves us so that He did not spare the life of His own Son, but delivered Him up for us all (Romans 8:32). In being delivered up for us all, Jesus intercedes for us all, not only in what He did, but also in what He said. First He said, "Father, forgive them, for they do not know what they do" (Luke 23:34), then to a penitent thief He says, "Assuredly, I say to you, today you will be with Me in Paradise" (Luke 23:43). From the lips of Jesus these words express the heart of God for one who is remorseful for his sins and for one who acknowledges the divinity of Jesus, even as the humanity of Jesus is dying next to him on a cross. The thief's request, "Remember me when You come into Your Kingdom" (Luke 23:42, NIV), summarizes the reason Jesus came. Jesus came "to seek and to save the lost" (Luke 19:10, NIV). Jesus came to redeem. Jesus came to recover. Jesus came to liberate. Jesus came to invite sinners into the Family of God, no matter the crime and no matter the allegation.

No matter the crime and no matter the allegation, still God loves us. No matter the crime and no matter the allegation, still God desires us to be with Him. Second Peter 3:9 emphasizes God's desire: "The Lord is not slack concerning His promise, as some count slackness, but is longsuffering toward us, not willing that any should perish but that all should come to repentance." Repentance is the requirement for salvation. Repentance is the only precondition of salvation. Regardless of the crime and regardless of the allegation the Bible says, "If we confess our sins, He [God] is faithful and just to forgive us our sins and to cleanse us from all unrighteousness" (1 John 1:9). Repentance is a two-step process. Confession is the first step of repentance; the other step involves a personal commitment from us to change our way of life. In combination, confession and conversion is repentance. In other words, repentance is a willingness to admit sin and to quit sin. In other words, it is the acknowledgement of sin in conjunction with the abdication of sin. Abdication means you give sin up. A failure or refusal to give up sin nullifies the validity of repentance.

In the second words of Jesus from the cross we learn that it is never too late to repent. In the second words of Jesus from the cross we learn that as long as we have physical life salvation is possible. This is not to say that we should wait and give a deathbed confession, but simply to say that it is never too late to acknowledge the Sonship of Jesus and never too late to be saved from the penalty of our sins. *Never too late* does not give us permission to procrastinate, for procrastination can prove fatal. Procrastination is "the action of delaying or postponing something." It means to defer. It means to reschedule. It means to suspend. It means to put off. Putting off a decision to accept Jesus is playing Russian Roulette with your soul. Tomorrow is not promised to any of us and none of us know when we will leave here. Putting off is not a wise choice. In contrast, the safe choice is NOW. In Second Corinthians 6:2 it is written, "Now is the accepted time; behold, now is the day of salvation."

We should never use the second conversation of the cross as an excuse to delay. The thief on the cross was blessed to have Jesus hanging next to him on a cross, but Jesus has already hung; He will not hang anymore, so do not procrastinate. NOW is the time to set our house in order. NOW is the time to get our lives right with God. NOW is the time to acknowledge Jesus and to accept Jesus. NOW is the time to decide between life and death, which is a decision of Heaven or Hell. We must decide now because Heaven awaits. We must decide now because Paradise is available. Paradise is a place of contentment. Paradise is a land of ultimate happiness. Unlike this world, in Paradise there is only peace, prosperity, and pleasure. Unlike this world, in Paradise there is no pain, sorrow, or suffering. In Paradise the death angel has no visitation rights. In Paradise there are no cemeteries, funeral homes, hospitals, or morgues. Paradise is a holy place. Paradise is a higher habitation. It is where God is. It is where Jesus is. It is where light is always present and darkness does not exist. Paradise is where the wicked cease from troubling and the weary are at rest.

The Garden of Eden was once our paradise, but we lost it, we gave it up, we were banished from it because we sinned. In the Garden of Eden, we disobeyed God. In the Garden of Eden, we violated God's will. In the Garden of Eden, we defied God's commandments. In the Garden of Eden, we listened to snake talk (Genesis 3). After God created this world, all that He created was good; no defects, no flaws, no disorder, and no immorality. But because we yielded to snake talk, we brought chaos to this world. We brought calamity to this world. We brought disease to this world. We brought perversion to this world. We brought death into this world. The condition of this world is not God's fault; we did it. But even though death came because of us, Jesus came to give us life (Romans 5:12-19). Jesus came to restore us. Jesus came to reinstate us. Jesus came to make us righteous again. Jesus came to give us anew what we dismantled through our choice to make the wrong choice. The wrong choice can mess up your world.

On the cross with Jesus were two thieves. One made the right choice. One made the wrong choice. On the cross with Jesus were two thieves. One criticized Jesus, the other defended Jesus. On the cross with Jesus were two thieves. One propositioned Jesus, "If You are the Christ, save Yourself and us" (Luke 23:39), the other entreated Jesus, "Lord, remember me when You come into Your Kingdom" (Luke 23:42). On the cross with Jesus were two thieves. One joined the crowd in mocking Jesus. One ignored the crowd and put his trust in Jesus. Both were crucified with Jesus, but one died in his sin, while the other was delivered from sin. Two men on Calvary with Jesus, one bound for Hell, the other blessed with Paradise. Destiny is based on choice. Both were criminals. Both deserved death. Both had opportunity, but only one took advantage. Only one saw Jesus as something more than just a man. Only one had faith in Jesus that changed his destiny. Make the right choice! The right choice is Jesus. He is "the Way, the Truth, and the Life" (John 14:6). In Jesus there is mercy. In Jesus there is grace. In Jesus there is forgiveness. Through Jesus awaits another chance. It is never too late for another chance, no matter the crime, no matter the allegation. All it takes is confession. All it takes is acknowledgement.

In Scripture the question is asked, "What must I do to be saved" (Acts 16:30)? In Scripture the answer is given, "Believe on the Lord Jesus Christ, and you will be saved" (Acts 16:31). It is not too late! One thief lost out, but one thief was invited in. Both had opportunity and both had done wrong, but while one railed on Jesus, the other thief repented. He admitted his guilt and says to Jesus: "Remember me" (Luke 23:42). Jesus gave him more than he asked for. More than remembrance he received redemption. More than remembrance he received forgiveness. More than remembrance he received salvation. More than remembrance he received Paradise. "Now to Him who is able to do exceedingly abundantly above all that we ask or think" (Ephesians 3:20). It is never too late!

The word from this word is: even the worst of sinners can be saved; no matter what, when, or where. "Jesus went to Calvary to save a wretch like you and me" (No Greater Love, GMWA National Mass Choir). It is never too late! But do not wait or procrastinate, accept Jesus now! But do not wait or procrastinate, the door of the Church is open now! The word is 'NOW!' Do it now! Come now! Confess now! Believe now! If you believe now, you receive now! If you believe now, Paradise is yours! New life is yours! Redemption is yours! Restoration is yours! Liberation is yours! Forgiveness is yours! Eternal Life is yours! It is not too late! It is never too late! Jesus says, "TODAY YOU WILL BE WITH ME IN PARADISE" (Luke 23:43). This is the purpose of the cross. This is the reason Jesus died. The word is NOW! "'Come now, and let us reason together,' says the LORD, 'though your sins are like scarlet, they shall be as white as snow; though they are red like crimson, they shall be as wool'" (Isaiah 1:18). It is not too late! It is never too late! Do not delay. Paradise can be yours!

"Now there stood by the cross of Jesus His mother, and His mother's sister, Mary the wife of Clopas, and Mary Magdalene. (26) When Jesus therefore saw His mother, and the disciple whom He loved standing by, He said to His mother, 'WOMAN, BEHOLD YOUR SON!' (27) Then He said to the disciple, 'BEHOLD YOUR MOTHER!' And from that hour that disciple took her to his own home."

John 19:25-27

Chapter Three

Woman, Behold Your Son

Behold Your Mother

(Theme: FAMILY RESPONSIBILITY)

As we continue examining the words of Jesus as spoken from the cross, once again we gather at Calvary and as we gather at Calvary we are looking up and beholding our Savior on a cross, and as we look up we hear Him once again speak from the cross. Seven times Jesus speaks. We have already examined His first and second words in chapters one and two. The focus of this chapter is on the third phrase that Jesus utters as He hangs on a cross dying a vicarious death for the sins of the world. The term vicarious conveys the idea of something being performed, received, or suffered in the place of someone else. As it has to do with Jesus and as it has to do with us, in hanging on the cross Jesus was being punished as a substitute for us. As the prophecy of Isaiah declares: "He was wounded for our transgressions, He was bruised for our iniquities" (Isaiah 53:5). On the cross at Calvary, Jesus "bore our sins in His body" (1 Peter 2:24). On the cross at Calvary, Jesus took our place. On the cross at Calvary, Jesus endured our sorrow. On the cross at Calvary, Jesus encountered our shame. On the cross at Calvary, Jesus died our death. But before He yields His spirit into the hands of His Father, seven times Jesus communicates from the cross and every expression has a purpose, every expression has a message, every expression has a lesson. The message and the lesson of His first words is forgiveness. The message and the lesson of His second words is salvation. The second words underscore that as long as there is physical life it is never too late to be saved.

As we are granted, through Scripture, the privilege of being near the cross, we look up again at Jesus. As we look up again at Jesus, Jesus is looking down at us from the cross and He beholds Mary, His mother. She is at the foot of the cross looking up weeping. Mary weeps, as any mother would weep, as she watches her son being crucified, suffering the most excruciating form of death. Crucifixion was a method of slow and painful execution in which the victim was tied or nailed to a large wooden cross and left there hanging for several days until he or she would eventually die from exhaustion and asphyxiation. Death by crucifixion was often performed in order to terrorize and dissuade others from perpetrating certain crimes. Those who were crucified were left on display even after death as a warning to others who might attempt the same about the fate that awaited them. Crucifixion was intended to provide a death that was gruesome, and a death that was humiliating, and a death that was intensely horrendous, and a death that was publicly reprehensible to both endure and observe.

Despite the many beautiful depictions of Jesus' death on a cross that are on display around the world, the crucifixion of Jesus was not a beautiful sight. Even before they crucified Jesus, they had already severely beaten Jesus, and scourged Jesus, and scarred Jesus, and spat upon Jesus, and slapped Jesus, and stripped Jesus of His clothing and of His dignity. Then He was made to carry His own cross to the site of crucifixion until He fell under the weight of the cross along the way (Mark 15:21). Already, before Calvary, physically weary and fatigued. Already, before Calvary, battered and bleeding. Already before Calvary, they placed a crown of thorns on His head. Then at Calvary, they put Him upright for all to see and Roman soldiers nailed His hands to the beam of the cross and did the same to His feet. No mother should behold such brutality being inflicted upon her child. No mother should have to see her child suffer. No mother should have to witness her child in agony. No mother should ever have to watch her child die, whether it be from sickness or disease, or from the senseless violence permeating our streets, or at the hands of individuals whose hatred towards her child would incite them to crucify Him without cause. But there at the cross of Calvary was Mary, the mother of Jesus, with a broken heart and with tears flowing from her eyes. Jesus was her first-born (Luke 2:7). Jesus was her miracle baby. Jesus was the one given to Mary through the intervention of the Holy Spirit (Luke 1:26-38). Mary had other children after Jesus with Joseph her husband (Matthew 12:46-50, 13:55; Mark 6:3; Luke 8:19; John 2:12, 7:3-10; Acts 1:14), but Joseph had nothing to do with the conception of Jesus. With Jesus Mary had an unparalleled bond. With Jesus Mary had a supernatural connection (Luke 1:26-38). But now Mary is at the cross and Jesus is dying. But even as life is leaving His earthly body, Jesus does not forget Mary. Even as life is leaving His earthly body, Jesus executes His obligation as her first-born.

In the law and custom of the Jews, the first-born son was considered the principle heir. In this, the first-born son would receive a double portion of his father's inheritance, or twice as much as any other son, or sons the father would have (Deuteronomy 21:15-17). As the first-born son it would be Jesus' responsibility to assume the responsibilities of the head of the household in the absence of His father. By father, we mean His earthly father Joseph. At the time of Jesus' crucifixion Mary was a widow. According to theological tradition, at some point during the course of the thirty-three years of Jesus' life Joseph had passed away which transferred the care of Mary to Jesus. So even while dying Jesus takes the time to make sure that Mary would be taken care of. Even after His resurrection three days after His death, 40 days later Jesus would ascend from earth to Heaven, back to the place from where He had come. In the absence of Joseph, Jesus would no longer be available to serve as the head of the household. Mary needed someone to provide for her. Mary needed someone to look after her.

In Scripture, the last time Joseph is mentioned is when Jesus was 12 years old (Luke 2:40-52). Eighteen years later, when Jesus began His earthly ministry at the age of 30, the name of Joseph is mentioned in lineage (Matthew 1:16), but not mentioned as being present at the baptism of Jesus, nor at any other event throughout the ministry of Jesus. Mary, His mother, is mentioned, and even His brothers and sisters are mentioned, but not Joseph (Matthew 12:46-50, 13:55; Mark 6:3; Luke 8:19; John 2:12, 7:3-10; Acts 1:14). Mary and the siblings of Jesus are cited as being present at a wedding in Cana of Galilee, where Jesus performs His first recorded miracle of turning water into wine, but not Joseph (John 2:1-11). Had Joseph been alive, certainly he would have been there because this was the wedding of a friend or relative of the family, and if Joseph were there I am certain his name would be included in the narrative of John Chapter 2. Even when Jesus returns to His hometown of Nazareth and teaches in a synagogue, He is referred to as "the carpenter, the son of Mary, the brother of James, and Joses, and of Judas and Simon," with no mention of Joseph (Mark 6:1-3). There is mention in Mark Chapter 6 that Jesus had sisters, but no mention of Joseph. Therefore, it is obvious that Joseph had died before this point. Even at the cross of Jesus, along with Mary is listed her sister Salome (Mark 15:40), Mary the wife of Cleophas (John 19:25), and Mary Magdalene (John 19:25), but there is no mention of Joseph. Had Joseph been alive he would have been there and his name would be mentioned. So we deduce from the omission of his name that Joseph was dead and

Jesus, as the first-born son, became the head of his household.

Jesus, being the first-born son, had the obligation to care for His parents when they got old, or to care for His mother in the event of His earthly father's death. Thus, as He is dying, Jesus sees to it that Mary would be cared for in His absence. Oh that children of today would learn from Jesus. Oh that sons and daughters of today would listen to the teachings of Jesus before the cross and to His words of wisdom from the cross. If we would do so, our parents would not be abused and neglected in nursing homes and senior citizen facilities. If we would do so, our parents would live out their final days surrounded by people who love them and surrounded by people who would not take advantage of them. In this world there are people who prey, P-R-E-Y, on our parents in their old age. In this world there are people who target our parents in their old age.

You never go wrong making sure mother is cared for. It is the will of God that mother be cared for. Like Jesus, you do not put mother into the wrong hands of care, or entrust mother's care into the hands of just anybody. Who Jesus selects He could trust. Who Jesus selects He knew would be one that would love Mary as his own mother. Who Jesus selects is "the disciple whom He loved" (John 19:26), and this disciple was John. At the foot of the cross with Mary, and with Mary's sister, and with Mary the wife of Cleophas, and with Mary Magdalene was John. Jesus loved John and John loved Jesus. John was Jesus' choice because Jesus knew that John was the right choice.

It is interesting to note that Jesus does not designate any of His brothers to be Mary's caretaker because His brothers and His sisters did not believe in Him (John 7:2-5) beyond Jesus simply being their brother. As Jesus hangs on the cross, His brothers and His sisters had not yet been 'born again.' It would come later, but not now, and Jesus was concerned about now. Now John was at the cross with Mary. At the cross there is no mention of Jesus' brothers or His sisters, but John was there. John was also family. John was Jesus' cousin, the son of Mary's sister Salome (Mark 15:40; Matthew 27:56), but the fact that he was Jesus' cousin was not the reason that John was chosen. John was chosen because John had been with Jesus. John was chosen because John had been taught by Jesus. John was chosen because John had been faithful to Jesus, and Jesus knew that John would be faithful to Mary. So Jesus hanging on the cross looks down and says to Mary, "Woman, behold your son" (John 19:26), and to John He says, "Behold your mother" (John 19:27) and the text says, "from that hour that disciple took her to his own home" (John 19:27). Tradition has it that John cared for Mary until the day that Mary died. Tradition has it that John loved Mary until the day she died.

What is the lesson of this text? The lesson is: Do not forget about mother. What is the message of Jesus' words? The message is: 'Take care of your mother.' Make sure that mother is provided for. Make sure that mother is taken care of. It does not have to be Mother's Day, but as long as you still have mother, you ought to do what you can for mother. Do not wait until May, every day ought to be Mother's Day. Do not wait until June, every day ought to be Father's Day. The first commandment with a promise is that we honor both father and mother (Exodus 20:12; Ephesians 6:2). The promise is: longevity of life. The promise is: prosperity in life. If you do what you can do as a son or as a daughter to bring delight to your parents, and to bring peace to your parents, and to bring comfort to your parents, and to put a smile on your parent's face, as well as joy in your parent's heart, then God is made happy and God will bless your life. God will add years to your life and bring contentment to your life. Always remember: 'what we sow, we reap' (Galatians 6:7). If you take care of your parents, your children will care for you, and if your children will not, I still believe that God will have somebody that will watch over you as you grow old and who will care for you when you get old. Even dying Jesus says, "Woman, behold your son" (John 19:26) and to John, "Behold your mother" (John 19:27)!

The word in this word is: RESPECT. The word in this word is: CARE. The word in this word is: LOVE. The word in this word is: FAMILY RESPONSIBILITY. Ephesians 6:1 declares, "Children, obey your parents in the Lord; for this is right." As a son or as a daughter, do your part to make your parents proud. As a son or as a daughter, do your part to make your parents happy. As a son or as a daughter, do your part to secure your parents. As a son or as a daughter, do your part to help your parents live. Do not cuss out mother. Do not disrespect mother. Do not disobey mother. Please, do not put your mother away. Your mother took care of you, wiped your nose and your butt, so take care of mother. Honor mother. Honor father. Honor precipitates honor. If you honor mother and father, God will honor you. If you see about mother and father, God will see about you. The word is: APPRECIATE! The words are: PROTECT and PROVIDE! The words are: BLESS THEM and RESPECT THEM! The words are: PUT A SMILE ON YOUR PARENTS' FACE and JOY IN THEIR HEART! Make today and every day Mother's Day! Make today and every day Father's Day! If you still have one or both, love them! If you still have one or both, make the rest of their lives the best of their lives! The word is: FAMILY TAKES CARE OF FAMILY!

"Now from the sixth hour until the ninth hour there was darkness over all the land. [46] And about the ninth hour Jesus cried out with a loud voice, saying, 'Eli, Eli, lama sabachthani?' that is, 'MY GOD, MY GOD, WHY HAVE YOU FORSAKEN MEN?'"

Matthew 27:45-46

Chapter Four

My God, My God,

Why Have You Forsaken Me?

(Theme: PROPITIATION & ATONEMENT)

As we continue standing around the cross of Calvary, it is the afternoon of the day and Jesus has been hanging for six hours. From the third to the present hour Jesus has spoken three times. The first time He intercedes for forgiveness. The second time He grants a penitent thief salvation and placement in Paradise. On the third time He entrusts the care of His mother Mary to His beloved disciple John, who takes Mary from the cross to his home to do as Jesus requested of him; He takes care of Mary for the rest of her natural life. As we continue to stand at the cross of Calvary darkness has eclipsed the sun for three hours. The darkness moment in human history occurs "from the sixth hour until the ninth hour" (Matthew 27:45).

At Calvary, Jesus, the Son of God, was being crucified. At Calvary, Jesus, the Son of God, was being tormented and executed at the hands of evil men. At the hands of evil men who hated Him. At the hands of evil men who were jealous of Him. At the hands of evil men who falsely accused Him. At the hands of evil men who were glad to see Jesus suffer and die simply because they wanted to be rid of Him. At Calvary, we see God at His best. At Calvary, we see man at his worst. At Calvary, we see the mercy and grace of God, but we also see the ruthlessness of mankind. At Calvary, we see Jesus doing what He was sent here to do. In contrast, at Calvary, on man's part what happened was murder. On the cross was Innocence, but it was Innocence dying for the guilty. On the cross was the fulfillment of God's will, in spite of mankind's rejection of God's will and God's way. Isaiah 53:6 says, "We all, like sheep, have gone astray, each of us has turned to our own way; and the LORD has laid on Him the iniquity of us all" (NIV).

The reason we see Jesus on the cross is because we, in essence, turned our backs on God. On the cross, Jesus was being wounded for our transgressions (Isaiah 53:5). On the cross, Jesus was being bruised for our iniquities (Isaiah 53:5). Jesus Himself had done nothing wrong. Jesus Himself had no sin in Him. But as the Apostle Paul declares in Second Corinthians 5:21, "God made Him who had no sin to be sin for us," and God did so because God loves us (John 3:16; Romans 5:8), and God did so because God could not and would not give up on us. The testimony of Second Peter 3:9 is that God "is not willing that any should perish." Although we deserve to die, in place of us God's Son would die. Although we deserve to die, in place of us Jesus would die so we could live. Although we deserve to die, in place of us Jesus would die to spare us the judgment of permanent death. At Calvary, the punishment that would bring us resurrection and peace was put on Him, and the punishment was so severe it caused a schism in the eternal union of *Father* and *Son*. A *schism* is a split or rupture; it is a separation or division into factions. On Calvary, like no other pain was the pain of divine disconnection. On Calvary, like no other pain was the pain that Jesus experienced when on the cross He bore our sins in His body.

The reason Jesus cries out for the fourth time from the cross uttering in agony, "My God, My God, why have You forsaken

Me" (Matthew 27:46), is because on the cross *God* is separating from *God*. In all of eternity this is the first and only time there is a break from divinity, leaving the humanity of Jesus on the cross to endure the full weight of the cross by Himself. By Himself, because God can have no communion with sin. By Himself, without the fellowship of His Father in Heaven. Without the fellowship of His Father in Heaven Jesus does not cry out Father, but God. This is the first and only time recorded that Jesus does not refer to God as Father. Here on the cross, quoting Psalm 22:1 Jesus says, "My God, My God, why have You forsaken Me" (Matthew 27:46). Two other times on the cross Jesus speaks to God, but even in those times He refers to God as Father. "Father, forgive them, for they do not know what they do" (Luke 23:34) and "Father, 'into Your hands I commit My spirit'" (Luke 23:46), but not this time. This time it is not Father, but God, and Jesus says "My God" twice because the fracture of fellowship was real. This time it is not Father because between "Father, forgive them, for they do not know what they do" (Luke 23:34) and "Father, into Your hands I commit My spirit" (Luke 23:46), the Son had taken sin upon Himself and the Father had turned His Back on His Son.

Turning one's back is the act of ignoring someone by turning away. It means you refuse to help. It means you decline to be involved with the plight of someone else. At Calvary, God was turning His back on Jesus because we had turned our backs on God. At Calvary, God was turning His back on Jesus because we continue to turn our backs on God. We turn our backs on God every time we disobey Him. We turn our backs on God every time we disown Him. We turn our backs on God every time we take what belongs to God (Tithe, Leviticus 27:30) and spend it on ourselves. We turn our backs on God every time we sell Jesus out for monetary gain like Judas did. We turn our backs on God when we do not shelter the homeless. We turn our backs on God when we do not feed the hungry. We turn our backs on God when we do not clothe the naked. We turn our backs on God when we do not visit the sick. We turn our back on God every time we misrepresent God through the foolishness and wickedness of sin. And on the cross God turns His back on Jesus because we have turned our backs on God.

What Jesus was doing on the cross He was doing for us. What Jesus subjected Himself to on the cross He did it willingly for us. He did it because we needed help. He did it because we needed rescue. He did it because we needed intervention. He did it because we needed a Savior. So at Calvary the *Son of God* becomes the *Lamb of God*, who would take away the sin of the world (John 1:29). At Calvary, suspended on a cross by nails and by His love for us Jesus cries out with a loud voice, "Eli, Eli, lama sabachthani" (AY-lee, AY-lee, luh-MAH-sah-BAHK-tah-nee), interpreted: "My God, My God, why have You forsaken Me" (Matthew 27:46). On the cross Jesus was forsaken because our sins were in Him.

I cannot explain it, but at some point on the cross there is a transference of every immorality, and of every depravity, and of every indulgence, and of every offence, and of every iniquity, and of every debauchery, and of every crime, and of every indiscretion, and of every corruption, and of every wicked deed, and of every wicked thought, and of every wicked word, and of every failing we have ever had, or will ever have against God. I cannot pinpoint the exact moment when the transgressions of mankind, from generation to generation, were reassigned to Jesus, but when it did happen the wrath of God was poured out on Jesus and in that brief moment the Word that was with God, and the Word that was God, and the Word Who had become flesh was disengaged from God, as in that brief moment He who was sinless was injected and infected with sin. I cannot explain the mystery of 'sovereign departure,' but on the cross it did happen. On the cross there was a split of divinity and humanity. On the cross there was an alienation of spiritual and natural. On the cross the fusion of Heaven and earth and the fusion of God and man was dislocated.

On the cross Jesus did not cease to be the Son, but temporarily He did cease to know the intimacy of *Father* and *Son*. Temporarily, for us, the Son became estranged from the Father. Temporarily, for us, the Father could not look upon the Son. What Mary, Jesus' earthly mother, saw from the ground as she looked up, God, Jesus' Heavenly Father, could not witness from up above as He looked down. Though this was God's will, it was nevertheless too infuriating to view. What father could watch his son endure such? What father could see such and not intervene? But God, who is rich in mercy could not intervene because redemption was at stake. But God, who is rich in mercy could not intervene because our future with Him was in jeopardy. Our restoration was in jeopardy. Our salvation was in jeopardy. Our sanctification was in jeopardy. Our acquittal of the charges against us was in jeopardy. The verdict of Romans 6:23 is: "the wages of sin is death;" thus somebody had to pay, and that Somebody became Jesus who hung on the cross proxy for us. For us, Elvina Hall writes in song: "Jesus paid it all, all to Him I owe; sin had left a crimson stain, He washed it white as snow" (Jesus Paid It All), but it cost Jesus. It freed us, but it cost Jesus. It exonerated us, but it cost Jesus. It cost Jesus, not only His life, but costlier than His life, it cost Jesus a momentary interruption of what had never been severed. What had never been severed was the Godhead of Father, Son, and Holy Spirit. What had never been severed was the interconnectedness that existed in the Godhead between Father, Son, and Holy Spirit. From eternity all three were one, now, momentarily, there is a breach in the Godhead. Our redemption cost Jesus. Our salvation cost Jesus. Our liberation cost Jesus. God's grace toward us cost Jesus.

Judas had betrayed Jesus, but what Judas did does not compare to what Jesus felt when, while on the cross, His Father left. Peter had denied Jesus three times, but what Peter did does not compare to what Jesus felt when, while on the cross, His Father left. All disciples but John had abandoned Jesus, but what they did does not compare to what His Father did while on the cross. The abandonment of God hurt Jesus. The abandonment of God grieved Jesus. The abandonment of God discomforted Jesus. The abandonment of God was too much for Jesus to bear. In incarnation Jesus gave up divine glory (Philippians 2:6), but in crucifixion Jesus gives up divine union. In incarnation Jesus could handle the embodiment of our flesh, but in crucifixion the embodiment of our sins causes Jesus to cry out with a loud voice, "My God, My God, why have You forsaken Me?" With a loud voice Jesus screams. With a loud voice Jesus hollers. He screams and He hollers because the pain was so great.

Greater than the pain of when they whipped Jesus was the pain of separation. Greater than the pain of how they mocked Jesus was the pain of separation. Greater than the pain of what was done to humiliate Jesus, and to disparage Jesus, and to blemish Jesus, and to put Jesus to open shame was the pain of separation. What causes Jesus to cry out was more painful than the nails that were thrust through His hands and His feet, and more painful than the crown of thorns that was placed on His head. Though His body was mutilated. Though His clothes were stripped. Though His face was disfigured. Though His back was marred and scarred, still, no greater pain was the pain of not being able to feel the presence of His Father as Jesus hung on the cross with our sins in His entire body.

It was three o'clock and something happened. Jesus became

unclean. It was three o'clock and something happened. Jesus became defiled. It was three o'clock and something happened. Jesus became corrupt. It was three o'clock and something happened. Jesus became the Scapegoat who took our sins upon Himself. In that moment He was all alone. In that moment He was left alone. God's presence had departed. God's presence had moved out. In that moment He was empty. In that moment He was orphaned. In that moment He was deserted. In that moment Jesus was Fatherless. In the three o'clock hour the inexplicable had occurred. The God-Man was just man and He was man without God. Without God He was frustrated. Without God He felt rejected. Without God He felt neglected. Without God He was simply human. He was human with the weight of the world on His shoulders. He was human with the sins of the world in His body. What else could Jesus do but cry out. What else could Jesus say besides "My God, My God, why have You forsaken Me?" God did it because He loves us. God did it because He cares. God did it because He made us and had a plan for our lives.

Yes, we have failed God. Yes, we have disobeyed God. Yes, we have turned our backs on God, but still God loves us: "For God so loved the world, that He gave His only begotten Son, that whosoever believeth in Him should not perish, but have everlasting life" (John 3:16). "But God commendeth His love toward us, in that, while we were yet sinners, Christ died for us" (Romans 5:8). This is God's plan for our lives! God abandoned Jesus to keep us. God gave Jesus up to bring us up. He did it to give us new life. He did it to give us a new name. He did it to give us a new body. God did it so we could have, when we leave here, a new Home. God had us on His mind. Jesus had us on His mind. Men thought they took Jesus' life, but He laid it down for us. For us Jesus suffered. For us Jesus was separated. For us Jesus knew sorrow. For us Jesus bled out, He cried out, and He died. It was all done to Him for us! For us Jesus cries out: "Eli, Eli, lama sabachthani" (AY-lee, AY-lee, luh-MAH-sah-BAHK-tah-nee). For us Jesus cries out: "MY GOD, MY GOD, WHY HAVE YOU FORSAKEN ME?"

"After this, Jesus knowing that all things were now accomplished, that the Scripture might be fulfilled, saith, 'I THIRST.' [29] Now there was set a vessel full of vinegar: and they filled a sponge with vinegar, and put it upon hyssop, and put it to His mouth."

John 19:28-29

Chapter Five

I Thirst

(Theme: PROPHECY FULFILLMENT)

We stand once again under the cross of Christ witnessing, through the records of Scripture, Jesus fulfilling the will of God as the Lamb of God. We stand once again near the cross as spectators in bewilderment at what our eyes are seeing and what our ears are hearing. We have been here at Calvary among the crowd observing Jesus in agony for six hours and listening to Jesus speak four times. The first time Jesus spoke He intercedes on behalf of those who played a part in getting Him to the cross and for those who took part in nailing Him on that cross. The first time Jesus spoke we hear Him asking God to forgive them for their unawareness of what they were doing, and to forgive them for their unawareness as to who they were doing it to. The first time Jesus spoke He says, "Father, forgive them, for they do not know what they do" (Luke 23:34). The lesson for us from Word 1 is: God wants us to forgive others just as He has forgiven us for Christ's sake (Ephesians 4:32).

The second time Jesus spoke He speaks to a penitent thief who hung alongside of Jesus at Calvary. The second time Jesus spoke He extends to this thief grace and grants him a place in Paradise. Paradise is the place we long to see and the place where Jesus currently is seated at the right hand of His Father. Jesus is there preparing Paradise for all who confess and believe in Him. To the thief who requested that Jesus remember him Jesus says:

"Assuredly, I say to you, today you will be with Me in Paradise" (Luke 23:43). The lesson for us from Word 2 is: It is never too late to repent. The lesson for us from Word 2 is: It is never too late to seek Jesus. As we declared in Chapter Two: It is never too late to be saved.

The third time Jesus spoke it was to His mother, Mary, and to His beloved disciple, John, both of whom were at the foot of the cross. Mary was weeping as she looked up at Jesus. John, as well as others, were at the cross consoling Mary as she wept. In speaking to Mary and John, Jesus makes sure that Mary would be taken care of for the rest of her earthly existence, fulfilling His obligation as her first-born son by entrusting the care of Mary to John. To Mary Jesus says: "Woman, behold your son" (John 19:26). To John Jesus says: "Behold your mother" (John 19:27). The lesson for us from Word 3 is: Take care of mother. The lesson for us from Word 3 is: Make sure mother is provided for. The lesson is: Look out for mother because God blesses those who are a blessing to their mother.

The fourth time Jesus spoke it was during the most excruciating phase of His crucifixion, a time in which our sins were literally inserted into His body. This insertion of our sins caused a split in the eternal union of *Father* and *Son*, a split that had never been and a split that left the humanity of Jesus enduring the full weight of the cross and judgment of God by Himself. This detachment that had never been experienced triggered Jesus to cry out with a loud voice: "Eli, Eli, lama sabachthani" (AY-lee, AY-lee, luh-MAH-sah-BAHK-tah-nee), interpreted: "My God, My God, why have You forsaken Me" (Matthew 27:46)? The lesson for us from Word 4 is: God loves us so much that He was willing to turn His back on His own Son so He could, once again, open up His arms and Heavenly Home to us. Now from the cross Jesus speaks for the fifth time, and in this fifth time He declares His thirst in fulfillment of prophecy (John 19:28).

Here on the cross we have Jesus, 100 percent divine, but also 100 percent human. Here on the cross we have Jesus, fully God and fully Man in one Person. Here on the cross is He who made the hill on which the cross stood and yet, on this hill He is nailed to wood. It is a mystery beyond comprehension, but in fact it is reality. John Chapter One says: "In the beginning was the Word, and the Word was with God, and the Word was God. The same was in the beginning with God. All things were made by Him; and without Him was not anything made that was made" (John 1:1-3). John 1:14 says: "The Word was made flesh, and dwelt among us." In the Person of Jesus, we have the fusion of divinity and humanity. In the Person of Jesus, we see One so unique that His life cannot be explained by natural methods. As God He is Creator, the One responsible for all living things, but as Man He is birth into this world through the womb of a woman like you and I, with the exception of the exclusion of a man in His conception. Unlike us, His birth was a supernatural birth. Unlike us, He bore the DNA of no man. In Jesus is the merger of Heaven and earth. He is God, but also Man. As God He is *invisible*, or *spirit* (John 4:24), but as Man we saw Him, we touched Him, we were touched by Him (1 John 1:1), and we ate and drank with Him.

Like us, as Man, Jesus got hungry (Matthew 4:2). Like us, as Man, Jesus needed sleep (Mark 4:38). Like us, as Man, Jesus was subject to the elements around Him. Like us, as Man, Jesus had to walk to get from point A to point B. Like us He was tempted to sin, though He did not sin (Hebrews 4:15). Like us He could bleed, and He did bleed for us. Like us Jesus had human emotions. Jesus cried like us (John 11:35). Jesus laughed like us. Jesus felt pain like us. Jesus became thirsty like us. On the cross, with a parched tongue He says, "I thirst" (John 19:28).

On the cross, with a dehydrated body He says, "I thirst." Before Jesus was nailed to a cross He had been beaten severely. After being beaten He was made to carry the cross of His crucifixion to the place He would be executed. For six hours on the cross Jesus experienced substantial blood loss from the crown of thorns they had placed on His head, as well as from the nails they had thrust into His hands and feet. Physically, Jesus was exhausted. Physically, Jesus was drained and worn-out. Physically, Jesus was weak. Physically, Jesus was depleted. Yes, He was God, but Jesus was also Man. As God He met needs, but as Man He had needs. On the cross, after all things were now accomplished Jesus looks to the Roman soldiers and says, "I thirst."

From the cross seven times Jesus speaks. The first three statements were centered on others, but after Jesus is done with what He had to endure for us, the last three statements are focused on Him. With the last three statements the focus is on His body, and on His mission, and on His spirit. Having relinquished all of Himself in obedience to God, Jesus can now concentrate on Jesus, but even in this He continues to adhere to what was foretold about Him. In John 5:39 you can read where Jesus says: "You search the Scriptures, for in them you think you have eternal life; and these are they which testify of Me." In saying "I thirst," Jesus was fulfilling the Messianic prophecy of Psalm 69:21, which reads:

> "They also gave me gall for My food, and for My thirst they gave Me vinegar to drink."

The vinegar that was given to Jesus was a cheap and sour Roman wine and the provision of such at a crucifixion was customary. The vinegar mixture was provided to those who hung on a cross in order to dull their senses to the unbearable pain they were undergoing. In Chapter Three we alluded to the fact that crucifixion was the most tormenting form of capital punishment during the days of Jesus. We also mentioned that crucifixion was a method of slow and painful execution in which those crucified were left hanging for several days until the person crucified would eventually die from exhaustion and asphyxiation. It only took Jesus six hours to die, but that is because His life was not taken from Him; instead, Jesus gave His life willingly for us. In John 10:18 He says: "No one takes it from Me, but I lay it down of Myself. I have power to lay it down, and I have power to take it again. This command I have received from My Father." Still, Jesus being human, the weight of the cross was taxing on His mind, and on His spirit, and on His body. Thus, after Jesus had fulfilled the Father's will of propitiation and salvation, now Jesus accomplishes what had been prophesied in Scripture as to what He would be given to drink.

It is interesting to note that when they first nailed Jesus to the cross, according to Matthew 27:34 and Mark 15:23, the Roman soldiers put vinegar mixed with some form of drug to Jesus' mouth. After tasting it, however, Jesus refused it. The question is: "Why did Jesus initially refuse the drink but makes a request for it now?" Again, the drink offered to Jesus was a cheap and sour Roman vinegar wine that was mixed with a drug to dull His senses. The Matthew account calls it "gall" (Matthew 27:34). The Mark account calls it "Myrrh" (Mark 15:23). It might help to know that both gall and myrrh are bitter medicinal herbs that are supposed to relieve pain. Again, it was the custom of the Romans to offer such to a person being crucified so the person crucified could more easily endure the pain of the cross. The reason Jesus refused it at first is because Jesus wanted to endure His suffering for us with a clear mind. For us He wanted to be conscious and alert about what was being done to Him and to what was going on around Him. For us He wanted to be conscious and alert enough to ask His Father for forgiveness on behalf of us (Luke 23:34) and conscious and alert enough to bring salvation to a repentant thief (Luke 23:43). For us He wanted to be conscious and alert enough to fulfill His obligation as Mary's first-born son (John 19:26-27) and conscious and alert enough to fulfill the prophecy of Scripture. For these reasons Jesus initially rejects the offer of vinegar mixed with gall or myrrh. However, as He nears death, having fulfilled all else but the prophecy of Psalm 69:21, He who is 'Living Water' and He who once said, "If anyone thirsts, let him come to Me and drink" (John 7:37), now says to others, "I thirst."

Jesus says "I thirst" because in His weakness He still had two more things to say and His mouth and throat needed moisture to say what needed to be said. Before this He had cried out with a loud voice, "My God, My God, why have You forsaken Me" (Matthew 27:46), and He could not say "It is finished" (John 19:30) until He first said, "I thirst." Jesus could not say, "Father, 'into Your hands I commit My spirit'" (Luke 23:46) until He first said, "I thirst." Thus, in fulfillment of Scripture Jesus says, "I thirst." When Jesus said, "I thirst," the record is: "They filled a sponge with sour wine, put it on hyssop, and put it to His mouth" (John 19:29). Now it was done. Now it was completed. Jesus had crossed every 'T' and dotted every 'I' of His Father's will and prophecy concerning Him.

All that the Father had given Jesus to do He had done. All that Scripture said that Jesus would do was fulfilled. It was now time to die. It was now time for Jesus to surrender His life. He had been wounded for our transgressions. He had been bruised for our iniquities. The worst was over and the best was yet to come! Soon He would be put in a tomb. Soon He would be raised from the dead. Soon we would see Him again. Soon the Son would return to His Father. Soon He would send the Holy Ghost to indwell us. Soon the Holy Ghost would empower us. Soon the Church would be born. Soon the Gospel would be told; the Gospel that saves lives; the Gospel that offers hope; the

Gospel that brings deliverance; the Gospel of transformation and regeneration. We would have no Gospel had Jesus not hung on the cross. We would have no Gospel had Jesus not died on that cross in our place. Thank God that He did. Thank God that Jesus said, "I thirst." Never deny the reality that God did come in the flesh. Never deny the reality that Jesus is Emmanuel, God with us (Matthew 1:23).

Jesus was God, but Jesus was also human. Jesus is God, but Jesus is also Man. He is the God-Man who knows our every pain. He is the God-Man who knows our every sorrow. He is the God-Man who knows our every hurt. He is the God-Man who knows the difficulties of our lives. Jesus is our Sympathetic Savior. Jesus is our Sacrificial Lamb. He came to do for us what we could not do for ourselves. He came to get back for us what we gave up because of sin. For us He put on flesh. For us He denied Himself. For us He humbled Himself. For us Jesus served. For us He was lied on. For us He was humiliated. For us He was scarred and disfigured. For us Jesus remained silent before His accusers. For us Jesus suffered. For us Jesus was separated. For us Jesus bore our sins. For us Jesus bled out and put His spirit in the Father's hands. He did it for us!

For us Jesus said, "Father, forgive them" (Luke 23:34). For us Jesus opened the doors to Paradise (Luke 23:43). For us Jesus showed us how to care for mother (John 19:26-27). For us Jesus cried out in anguish, "My God, My God, why have You forsaken Me" (Matthew 27:46). After everything had been accomplished Jesus then said, "I thirst." What more does God have to do? What more could God do? God did not spare His own Son, but gave Him up for us (Romans 8:32). Here is the report: "For God so loved the world that He gave His only begotten Son, that whoever believes in Him should not perish but have everlasting life" (John 3:16).

Lest we forget, we are at Calvary, the place of God's grace. Lest we forget, we are at Calvary, the place of God's mercy. Lest we forget, we are at Calvary, the place of God's forgiveness. Lest we forget, we are at Calvary, the place where God has given us another chance. In his song, "The Old Rugged Cross," George Bennard wrote: "On a hill far away stood an old rugged cross, the emblem of suff'ring and shame; and I love that old cross where the Dearest and Best, for a world of lost sinners was slain. So I will cherish the old rugged cross, till my trophies at last I lay down; I will cling to the old rugged cross; and exchange it someday for a crown." Someday because God loves us. Someday because God cares. Someday because God put Himself in harm's way. Someday because Jesus died for us! Because Jesus died for us, we shall live again. Because Jesus died for us, no grave will keep us down. Because Jesus died for us, this world is not our home. Because Jesus laid down His life for us, we should lay down our lives for Him. Lest we forget, Jesus thirst for us, now let us thirst for Him. Let us live for Him. Let us tell His story. Let us bring Him glory. Let us bear our own cross. With His fifth expression from the cross Jesus said: "I THIRST." With my thirst I state the longing of the psalmist: "As the deer pants for the water brooks, so pants my soul for You, O God" (Psalm 42:1). Are you thirsty? Jesus said: "Blessed are those who hunger and thirst for righteousness, for they shall be filled" (Matthew 5:6).

"So when Jesus had received the sour wine, He said, 'IT IS FINISHED!' And bowing His head, He gave up His spirit."
John 19:30

Chapter Six

It Is Finished

(Theme: MISSION ACCOMPLISHED)

We are gathered at a place just outside of the city walls of Jerusalem. It is a place called in the Hebrew tongue of Aramaic, GOLGOTHA, and in the Latin language of the Romans and Greeks, CALVARY. We are here because it is a place of crucifixion. We are here because it is a place where individuals guilty of crimes are put to death by the Roman government. We are here because on three crosses hang three men, two who have been charged with thievery and One who is charged with blasphemy. We do not know the names of the thieves, but the One hanging in the middle charged with blasphemy is Jesus. His crime, or the charge against Him, is that He claims to be the Son of God. But how can He be the Son of God and also the son of a carpenter? How can He be the Son of God crying out to God from a cross?

Above Jesus there is a sign with an inscription written in Hebrew, Greek and Latin that reads: "Jesus of Nazareth, the King of the Jews" (John 19:19-20). It is an inscription placed there by the order of Pontius Pilate, who is the Roman governor of Judea. It is an inscription that was designed to infuriate the Jewish religious leaders who brought Jesus to Pilate and who insisted that Jesus be put to death by Pilate. According to John 19:21, these religious leaders wanted Pilate to revise the sign to read: "He said, I am the King of the Jews," but Pilate said, "What I have written I have written" (John 19:22). Pilate found no fault in Jesus (John 19:4). Pilate washed his hands of Jesus (Matthew 27:24). But no way was Pilate exonerated for the part he played in the crucifixion of Jesus. Jesus was on a cross because Pilate consented to His death and handed Jesus over to be crucified. Could this crucified Jesus be the King of the Jews? Could this crucified Jesus be the Son of God dying on a piece of wood?

Indeed, He who hung on the middle cross was a King. Indeed, He who hung on the middle cross was the Son of God, the Christ, the Messiah of the Jews. It was He who had been promised before the foundation of the world. It was He who had been prophesied through Scripture would come. As promised, in the fullness of time Jesus did come (Galatians 4:4). As prophesied, Jesus was born of a virgin (Isaiah 7:14; Matthew 1:18). As prophesied, Jesus was born in Bethlehem (Micah 5:2; Matthew 2:1). As prophesied, Jesus was preceded by a messenger to prepare His way (Malachi 3:1; Matthew 11:7-11). As prophesied, Jesus was called out of Egypt (Hosea 11:1; Matthew 2:15). As prophesied, Jesus was referred to as a Nazarene (Judges 13:5; Amos 2:11; Lamentations 4:7; Matthew 2:23). As prophesied, Jesus was rejected by His own (Isaiah 53:3; Matthew 21:42; Mark 8:31, 12:10; Luke 9:22, 17:25). As prophesied, Jesus was betrayed by a friend (Psalm 41:9; John 13:21). As prophesied, Jesus was sold for 30 pieces of silver (Zechariah 11:12; Matthew 26:15; Luke 22:5). As prophesied, Jesus was forsaken by His disciples (Zechariah 13:7; Matthew 26:56). As prophesied, Jesus was accused by false witnesses (Psalm 35:11; Matthew 26:60). As prophesied, Jesus remained silent before His accusers (Isaiah 53:7; Matthew 27:14). As prophesied, Jesus healed the blind, the deaf, the lame, and the dumb (Isaiah 35:5-6, 29:18; Matthew 11:5). As prophesied, Jesus preached to the poor, the brokenhearted, and He set the captives free (Isaiah 61:1; Matthew 11:5). As prophesied, Jesus was spat upon, smitten, and scourged (Isaiah 50:6, 53:5; Matthew 27:26, 30). As prophesied, Jesus was hated without a cause (Psalm 35:19; Matthew 27:23). As prophesied, Jesus was wounded for our sins and bruised for our iniquities (Isaiah 53:5). As prophesied, Jesus was crucified with criminals (Isaiah 53:12; Matthew 27:35). As prophesied, Jesus was pierced in His side (Zechariah 12:10; Psalm 22:16), but not a bone of His body was broken (Psalm 34:20; Numbers 9:12; John 19:33-36). As prophesied, soldiers gambled for His garment (Psalm 22:18; Matthew 27:35). As prophesied, soldiers gave Jesus vinegar mixed with gall (Psalm 69:21; Matthew 27:34). As prophesied, Jesus cried out, "My God, My God, why have You forsaken Me" (Psalm 22:1; Matthew 27:46). As prophesied, there was darkness over the land (Amos 8:9; Matthew 27:45). As prophesied, He was buried with the rich (Isaiah 53:9; Matthew 27:57, 60). As prophesied, He was resurrected from the dead (Psalm 16:10-11, 49:15; Mark 16:6). As prophesied, He ascended to the right hand of God (Psalm 68:18; Luke 24:51). As prophesied, His name is Emmanuel (Isaiah 7:14; Matthew 1:23). Jesus crossed every 'T' and dotted every 'I' of prophecy concerning Himself. There is no doubt He is a King. In fact, Jesus is the King of kings (Revelation 19:16). There is no doubt He is the Son of God. In fact, Jesus is the only begotten Son of God (John 3:16). Having done everything that He was assigned to do, the text says: "When Jesus therefore had received the vinegar, He said, 'It is finished'" (John 19:30). But the question before us is: What exactly had Jesus finished?

As discussed in previous chapters; Jesus was crucified on a cross in order to secure, for us, renewed fellowship with God. Because of sin we broke the fellowship we had with God. Because of sin we became estranged or alienated from God. When Adam and Eve disobeyed God in the Garden of Eden we were put at odds with God and banished from the utopia that God had created for us. The thought of utopia is the thought of a place or a state of things in which everything is perfect. Things are far from perfect now, but in the beginning when God created the heaven and the earth (Genesis 1), all things were perfect. When God blew into us the breath of life, we awakened to a world of sinless flawlessness. When God blew into us the breath of life, we awakened to a world of beauty and plenty and to a world of unity and pleasure. But we listened to snake talk and we messed it all up (Genesis 3). Therefore, into our mess God sent a Savior. Therefore, into our mess God dispatched Himself to be our Redeemer, Liberator, Debt Eradicator, and to be the One who would take upon Himself the punishment for us all.

In Chapter Five I mentioned that Jesus came to do for us what we could not do for ourselves. In Chapter Five I mentioned that Jesus came to get back for us what we gave up when we decided to trust ourselves instead of God. Self-trust is misplaced trust, and misplaced trust always takes us away from God. In other words, anytime we depend more on intellect than on divine inspiration and revelation, we position ourselves further and further outside of the will of God. In other words, anytime we look to psychics and horoscopes rather than read and comply with the Word of God, we position ourselves further and further outside of the will of God. Psalm 146:3-5 instructs us not to put our confidence in man but to hope in God. Proverbs 3:5-6 declares: "Trust in the LORD with all your heart, and lean not on your own understanding; in all your ways acknowledge Him, and He shall direct your paths."

Jesus came here for us. Jesus is on the cross for us. On the cross He is God's redemptive work for us because we needed redeeming from our submission and slavery to sin and Satan. Before the fall in the Garden of Eden, God had a plan in place for us because He knew before He created us that we would fail

Him. In other words, before God said, "Let there be" (Genesis 1:3), and before all that we are and all that we see came into being, God formulated a strategy to rescue us from sin and Satan's grip, and to resuscitate us from our fate of death. First Peter 1:20 says, "God chose Him as ransom long before the world began" (NLT). Revelation 13:8 refers to Jesus as "the Lamb who was slaughtered before the world was made" (NLT). The question is: What did Jesus finish?

As Christ, or as God in human flesh, Jesus put Himself in harm's way. As Christ, or as God in human flesh, Jesus allows Himself to be crucified under His own wrath, in our place, as a sacrifice for the sin we committed. For sin, blood has always been required by God, and the required blood for sin has always been innocent blood. From the Garden of Eden to the sacrificial system of the Mosaic Law, and from the sacrificial system of the Mosaic Law to the very cross of Jesus Christ, the price for sin is the price of blood. The songwriter, Robert Lowry, penned these lyrics: "What can wash away my sin? What can make me whole again? Nothing but the blood of Jesus." "Oh! Precious is the flow that makes me white as snow; no other fount I know, nothing but the blood of Jesus" (Nothing but the Blood). William Cowper wrote: "There is a fountain filled with blood drawn from Emmanuel's vein; and sinners plunged beneath that flood lose all their guilty stains" (There is a Fountain). Hebrews 9:22 states: "Without shedding of blood there is no remission." What did Jesus finish?

Jesus was sent here to destroy the works of the devil (1 John 3:8). Jesus was sent here to open the eyes of the blind (Luke 4:18). Jesus was sent here to call sinners to repentance (Luke 5:32). Jesus was sent here to preach the Gospel to the poor (Luke 4:18). He came here to heal the sick. He came here to revive the dead. He came here to offer hope. Jesus came here to bear witness unto the truth (John 18:37). He came here to redeem.

He came here to recover. He came here to reconcile. Jesus came here to resurrect dead lives. He came here to serve (Mark 10:45). He came here to do His Father's will. He came here to establish His church. Jesus came here to train men on how to be fishers of men. He came here to teach morals. He came here to model behavior. He came here to be light amidst darkness. Jesus came here to seek and to save the lost (Luke 19:10). He came here to fulfill prophecy. He came here to satisfy the Law (Matthew 5:17). He came here to reveal the Father. Jesus came here that we might have life, and that more abundantly (John 10:10). He came here to atone for sin (Hebrews 2:17). He came here to judge the world of sin (John 9:39). He came here to bridge the gap between us and God (1 Timothy 2:5). Jesus came here to die, in our place, on the cross (John 12:27). What did Jesus finish?

Jesus finished the work of securing for us peace with God and gaining for us amnesty for our transgressions against God. Jesus finished the work of blending Jew and Gentile into one body and of making God accessible to all of us. When Jesus died on the cross the veil of the Temple was torn in two, granting us entry, not once a year, but every day to the Throne of God's grace (Hebrews 4:16). He finished the work of forgiveness. He finished the work of sanctification. He finished the work of propitiation. He finished the work of salvation. I have been saying, from chapter to chapter, Jesus did for us what we could not do for ourselves. I have been saying, from chapter to chapter, Jesus gave back to us what we gave up through disobedience. Through disobedience we turned this world over to Satan, but through the obedience of Jesus we got it back. Through Jesus we regained fellowship. Through Jesus we regained Paradise. Through Jesus we regained immortality. Through Jesus we regained authority and dominion. Because of Jesus we have power again. Because of Jesus we have victory again. Because of Jesus we have joy again. Because of Jesus the grave has no sting. What did Jesus finish?

Jesus paid our price. Jesus suffered our sorrow. Jesus endured our pain. Jesus placated, or conciliated the wrath of God for us. For us "He was wounded" (Isaiah 53:5). For us "He was bruised" (Isaiah 53:5). For us "the chastisement for our peace was upon Him" (Isaiah 53:5). For us Jesus stayed the course of redemption until redemption became ours. We are free because of Jesus. We are whole because of Jesus. We are healed because of Jesus. Every sin charge has been dropped because Jesus deferred His will to God's will. What did Jesus finish? God promised one day to crush the head of the serpent through the seed of a woman (Genesis 3:15), and "when the set time had fully come" (Galatians 4:4, NIV), God did just that. God sent His Son into this world, "born of a woman, born under the law" (Galatian 4:4, NIV). Into this world God sent Jesus. Into this world God sent a Savior. He was wrapped in swaddling clothes and He was laid in a manger (Luke 2:12). He dwelt here for 33 years and for 3 of the 33 He healed the sick, raised the dead, gave sight to the blind, made the lame to walk, the mute to talk, fed the hungry, and Jesus served humanity. Everywhere Jesus went He preached the Gospel. Everywhere Jesus went He brought hope to the hopeless and life to the lifeless. Jesus taught us how to pray. Jesus showed us how to love. Jesus revealed to us our true neighbor. Jesus glorified God in all He did. What did Jesus finish?

Jesus finished our restoration. Jesus finished our reconciliation. Jesus finished our regeneration. Jesus finished what He was told by His Father to do. He came unto His own and His own rejected Him. His own ridiculed Him. His own despised Him. His own dishonored Him. His own betrayed Him. His own denied Him. His own abandoned Him. His own lied on Him.

His own beat Him. His own degraded Him. His own spat on Him. His own crucified Him. Men stripped Him of His garments. Men placed a crown of thorns on His head. Men nailed Jesus to a cross. Men lifted Him up for all to see. To sum it all up: JESUS DIED FOR OUR SINS! For this purpose, He was born. For this purpose, He let them do it. For this purpose, He endured the shame. For this purpose, Jesus felt the pain. "So when Jesus had received the sour wine, He said, 'It is finished!' And He bowing His head, He gave up His spirit" (John 19:30). All that Jesus did He did it for you and I. "Jesus went to Calvary to save a wretch like you and me" (No Greater Love, David Allen). "They hung Him high, they stretched Him wide. He hung His dead, for me He died" (No Greater Love, David Allen), but why did Jesus do it? He did it for love: "For God so loved the world that He gave His only begotten Son, that whoever believes in Him should not perish but have everlasting life" (John 3:16). This is the Gospel of Jesus Christ! This is the Good News of Salvation! Jesus stayed in redemption mode until redemption had been accomplished. When all had been accomplished, when all had been said and done Jesus said, "IT IS FINISHED!" Now the door of the Church is open! Now grace is available! Now mercy is in your reach! Now forgiveness is an option! Now new life can be yours! IT IS FINISHED!

"Now it was about the sixth hour, and there was darkness over all the earth until the ninth hour. [45] Then the sun was darkened, and the veil of the temple was torn in two. [46] And when Jesus had cried out with a loud voice, He said, 'FATHER, INTO YOUR HANDS I COMMIT MY SPIRIT.' Having said this, He breathed His last."

Luke 23:44-46

Chapter Seven

Father, Into Your Hands

I Commit My Spirit

(Theme: DIVINE TRUST)

As I write this final chapter, I write it in anticipation of Good Friday. Good Friday, along with Resurrection Sunday, is the apex of our Christian faith. Good Friday is the day in which Christians all around the world gather together in commemoration of the crucifixion of Jesus and of His death at Calvary. We commemorate the death of Jesus because His death provides us with life and because His death eradicated, or eliminated our sin debt to God. What we owed God, because of sin, was too much for us to pay. What God required for sin, by us, was too much for us to bear. So God prepared a body for Himself before the foundations of the world and in the time set by God, He came into this world to do for us what we could not do for ourselves. God came here to be our Scapegoat. God came here to be our Sacrificial Lamb. God came here to be our Atonement. God came here to hang proxy for us. While here, God, in the Person of Jesus, did many things such as: cured all manner of sicknesses and diseases. He gave sight to the blind. He enabled the lame to walk and the mute to talk. He fed the hungry. He raised the dead. He encouraged the discouraged and invited sinners, both Jew and Gentile, to the Throne of God's grace. But His ultimate purpose for coming was to give His life as a ransom for many (Mark 10:45). His ultimate purpose for coming was to yield His life to crucifixion for our sins (John 12:27).

Although I write this chapter in anticipation of Good Friday, I have been at Calvary for several weeks. I did not wait for Good Friday to get here in order to go there, but I have been here witnessing a horrendous sight and hearing a collection of conversations. I have been here watching people taunt Jesus. I have been here watching people berate Jesus. I have been here as the crowd mocked Jesus. I have been here as soldiers gambled for His garment. I have been here seeing blood ooze from Jesus' body. I have been here beholding blood flowing from His head, hands, and feet. I have been here as the sun was eclipsed for three of the six hours that Jesus hung on the cross, Matthew 27:45 declaring: "From the sixth to the ninth hour." At the foot of the cross I see Mary, the mother of Jesus, weeping for her son and being consoled by others: by her sister, and by Mary the wife of Cleopas, and by Mary Magdalene, and by Jesus' beloved disciple John (John 19:25-26). Who else was there I do not know, but Scripture lets us know that these three women were at the cross, along with John as Jesus was crucified. As Jesus was crucified, I hear Jesus speak seven times, three times on behalf of others, once because of divine separation, and the last three times concerning Himself. It is what Jesus voiced from the cross that drew me to the cross hearing Him say: "Father, forgive them, for they do not know what they do" (Luke 23:34), "Assuredly, I say to you, today you will be with Me in Paradise" (Luke 23:43), "Woman, behold your son" (John 19:26), "Behold your mother" (John 19:27), "My God, My God, why have You forsaken Me" (Matthew 27:46), "I thirst" (John 19:28), "It is finished" (John 19:30), and now "Father, 'into Your hands I commit My spirit'" (Luke 23:46). Now Jesus can once again call God Father because all that God had given Him to do was done. Every sin was judged. Every prophecy was fulfilled. Every soul had been redeemed. Satan's head had been crushed. Now the union of Father and Son had been restored. Now it was time for Jesus to be separated from His body. Now it was time for the earthly body of Jesus to become lifeless. Now it was time for Jesus, the Son of man, to die. But God had promised that He would raise Jesus up again. Before the cross the Father had promised the Son resurrection in three days. Now the Son puts His total trust in His Father as He prepares to breathe His last breath and surrender His spirit. Jesus surrenders His spirit; no one took His life. Jesus laid it down willingly for us (John 10:18). For us Jesus waives His right to life. For us, from the cross, one more time He cries out with a loud voice.

Having said, "Father, forgive them, for they do not know what they do" (Luke 23:34). Having said, "Assuredly, I say to you, today you will be with Me in Paradise" (Luke 23:43). Having said, "Woman, behold your son" (John 19:26) and "Behold your mother" (John 19:27). Having said, "My God, My God, why have You forsaken Me" (Matthew 27:46). Having said, "I thirst" (John 19:28). Having said, "It is finished" (John 19:30). The moment had arrived for Jesus to die. The moment had arrived for the human side of Jesus to depart this world. But dying was no surprise to Jesus. Dying was no bombshell of revelation to Jesus. Jesus knew He had to die. Jesus had already told His disciples that He would die. Before the cross He prophesied His death. Before the cross He prophesied His resurrection. Many times Jesus said to His disciples: "The Son of man will be delivered into the hands of men, and they shall kill Him; and after He is killed, He shall rise the third day" (Mark 9:31). No, death was no surprise to Jesus. No, death was no bombshell of revelation to Jesus. Jesus had to die so we could live. Jesus had to die in order to free us from the penalty and permanence of death.

In song Donald Vails wrote: "He would not come down from the cross just to save Himself. He decided to die just to save me" (He Would Not Come Down). Jesus would not come down in order to liberate us. Jesus would not come down in order to justify us. Jesus would not come down in order to exonerate us. Jesus would not come down in order to recover us. This is why Jesus came. This is why Jesus stayed here. This is why Jesus suffered. This is why Jesus died. Even in His death there is a lesson for us. Even in His final words from the cross there is a message for us. The lesson and the message are: TRUST GOD. The lesson and the message are: PUT YOUR LIFE IN GOD'S HANDS.

What better hands to put our lives in other than in the Hands of God? What better hands to put our trust in other than in the Hands of God? In the Hands of God is the place to be. In the Hands of God is where we need to be. In God's Hands is security. In God's Hands is safety. In God's Hands is protection. In God's Hands is shelter. In God's Hands is provision. In God's Hands is consolation. In God's Hands is peace. In God's Hands is love. In God's Hands is mercy. In God's Hands is grace. In God's Hands is forgiveness. In God's Hands is new life. In God's Hands is promise. In God's Hands is another chance. In God's Hands is divine support. In God's Hands is eternal life. There are no hands like God's Hands, for there is nobody like God. There is nobody who cares like God. There is nobody who will hold you like God. There is nobody who will keep you like God. There is nobody who will satisfy you like God. Revelation 14:13 says: "Blessed are the dead who die in the Lord."

In the Lord there is rest. In the Lord there is favor. In the Lord there is comfort. In the Lord there is a Watchful Eye. Jesus says: "Father, into Your hands I commit My spirit." Into Your hands I put My faith. Into Your hands I put My confidence. Into Your hands I put My will. Into Your hands I resign Myself. Lord, into Your hands I give up. Lord, into Your hands I yield. Lord, into Your hands I turn it all over. Lord, into Your hands I lay down My life. Lord, I surrender! Lord, I concede! I concede my life. I concede my love. I concede my heart. I concede my trust. "I will trust in the Lord until I die" (I Will Trust in the Lord, C.L. Franklin). Even as death approaches me, I will yet trust the Lord. What better hands to be in other than in the Hands of God? What better hands to defer to other than the Hands of God?

When life seems rough, when life gets tough, when life grows cold and your years turn old, put your life in God's Hands. When friends are few, when money is low, when death is calling and your tears begin to flow, put your life in God's Hands. In fact, no matter what comes your way, no matter what the situation is, keep your life in God's Hands. Hold on and do not let go. Hold on and hang in there. Although "time is filled with swift transitions" and "naught of earth unmoved can stand," "build your hopes on things eternal" and "hold to God's unchanging hand" (Hold to God's Unchanging Hand, Jennie B. Wilson). God is the same today as He was on yesterday. You can trust God. You can depend on God. You can lean on God. You can rely on His Word. There are no hands like God's Hands! There is no one like God! You too should say like Jesus said: "Father, into Your hands I commit My spirit." Father, in You I put my faith. Father, in You I put my confidence. Father, in You I put my will. Father, in You I resign myself. Lord, I give up! Lord, I yield! Lord, I turn it all over! Lord, I give You my life! The final word from the final Word is: TRUST GOD! The final word from the final Word is: KEEP YOUR HANDS IN GOD'S HANDS! God will never let you down. God will never abandon you. Put your life in God's hands! Keep your life in God's hands. In God's hands everything will be alright. We know that in God's hands death gives way to life and every cross has a crown. Like Jesus, we are in good hands with God. All I need to say is: "THREE DAYS LATER!"

Three Days Later!

"For as Jonah was three days and three nights in the belly of the great fish, so will the Son of Man be three days and three nights in the heart of the earth."

Matthew 12:40

I do not want to make the assumption that all who read this book have the awareness of what I make reference to when I ended my final chapter with the phrase: "THREE DAYS LATER!" When Jesus uttered His last word, "Father, 'into Your hands I commit My spirit'" (Luke 23:46), He breathed His last breath and died. Upon His death His body was taken down from the cross and placed in a tomb that was the property of a man by the name of 'Joseph of Arimathea.' *Joseph of Arimathea* was a member of the Sanhedrin Council, an assembly of seventy men that was comprised of priests, scribes, and elders. The Sanhedrin Council held judicial jurisdiction over the province of Judea. It was this Council that judged Jesus and condemned Him to death. It was this Council that handed Jesus over to the Roman Procurator, Pontius Pilate, and insisted that Jesus be crucified. Joseph of Arimathea was a member of this Council, however, he is described in Scripture as "a good and just man" (Luke 23:50) and as one who "had not consented to their decision and deed" (Luke 23:51).

Upon the death of Jesus, Joseph of Arimathea "went to Pilate and asked for the body of Jesus" (Luke 23:52). Upon consent, he took the body down from the cross, "wrapped it in linen, and laid it in a tomb that was hewn out of the rock" (Luke 23:53), the Bible says, "where no one had ever lain before" (Luke 23:53). This was done expeditiously because "the Sabbath drew near"

(Luke 23:54). The body of Jesus had not been properly prepared for burial as prescribed by Jewish law and custom, but it did not have to be because His burial was only temporary. Before His death, Jesus had prophesied His resurrection from the dead. On many occasions He talked of His crucifixion and death, but also of His resurrection. Note: Matthew 12:40, Matthew 16:21, Matthew 20:17, Mark 8:31, Luke 18:31-34, and John 2:19-22. I quote Matthew 12:40 under the title of this discussion, but let me state here the words of Mark 8:31:

"And He began to teach them that the Son of Man must suffer many things, and be rejected by the elders and chief priest and scribes, and be killed, and after three days rise again."

"THREE DAYS LATER" is reference to the resurrection of Jesus. Three days later women would arrive at the tomb of Jesus to anoint His body, only to discover that the tomb is empty and His body is not there (Luke 24:1-7). The body of Jesus was no longer in the tomb because Jesus had risen like He said He would. In stating "THREE DAYS LATER" we celebrate the assurance of God's promise and of His word. In stating "THREE DAYS LATER" we substantiate the security of one's life that is placed in the hands of God. As Jesus said, "Father, 'into Your hands I commit My spirit'" (Luke 23:46) with confidence that His life was in good hands and that "THREE DAYS LATER" life would be restored to His body as His Father had promised, so we can rest in the promise of God's Word when it says: "For if we believe that Jesus died and rose again, even so them also which sleep in Jesus will God bring with Him" (1 Thessalonians 4:13). "THREE DAYS LATER" culminates the Gospel story. "THREE DAYS LATER" authenticates the message of John 3:16: "For God so loved the world that He gave His only begotten Son, that whoever believes in Him should not perish but have everlasting life." "THERE DAYS LATER" lets us know that the suffering of Calvary was not in vain. Indeed, Jesus "was wounded for our transgression" (Isaiah 53:5). Indeed, Jesus "was bruised for our iniquities" (Isaiah 53:5). "THREE DAYS LATER" leaves no room for doubt that there are no better hands to be in other than IN GOD'S HANDS!

Epilogue

I have endeavored in this book to bring relevance to the words spoken by Jesus from the cross. I have endeavored to unveil the truth of each word, to exegete each word in order to bring clarity to why Jesus said what He said, and to echo the message communicated in each word for us. From the cross Jesus still teaches and from the cross there are still lessons to learn and apply. God still wants us to forgive others, as He forgives us for Christ's sake (Ephesians 4:32). God still wants others to know that salvation is possible, no matter the crime, indiscretion, or allegation. It is still God's will that we honor our parents (Exodus 20:12; Ephesians 6:2). It is still God's will that we fulfill His will. It is still God's will that we remain faithful unto death (Revelation 2:10). It is still in our best interest to put our lives in God's hands.

Jesus' seven expressions from the cross remain at the forefront of every Good Friday sermon, service, and celebration. Each expression still excites. Each expression still instructs. Each expression still inspires. Each expression still beckons us to the cross to hear, over and over again, our Savior interceding for others, welcoming a penitent thief into Paradise, entrusting the care of a mother into the arms of a beloved disciple, crying out with a loud voice in agony over divine disconnection, fulfilling the prophecy of Scripture by saying "I thirst," declaring the words of mission accomplished, and yielding His spirit into the hands of a loving and faithful God. I never grow tired of reexamination. I never grow tired of re-proclamation. There is still doctrine in each word. There is still revelation in each word. At Calvary, Jesus spoke from the cross and His words from the cross still speaks.

The seven communications of Jesus from the cross are awe-inspiring commentaries in His own words on the themes of forgiveness, salvation, family responsibility, propitiation, atonement, suffering, accomplishment, victory, and security. From Jesus' own lips we gage His heart, His humanity, His concern, His compassion, as well as His determination to complete His divine assignment. May we, like Jesus, give our lives for the betterment of others. May we, like Jesus, stay the course of sacrifice and submission, conceding our will to God's will. May we, like Jesus, trust God, obey God, and please God in every way. May we, like Jesus, use our words in life and our final words before death to bring hope, comfort, assurance, and direction to someone else. Jesus was nailed to a cross to bring redemption to us. He spoke from the cross still teaching us. May we bear our own crosses and may we glorify God in word and deed like Jesus did. His words from the cross still has something to say! The question is: Are we listening?

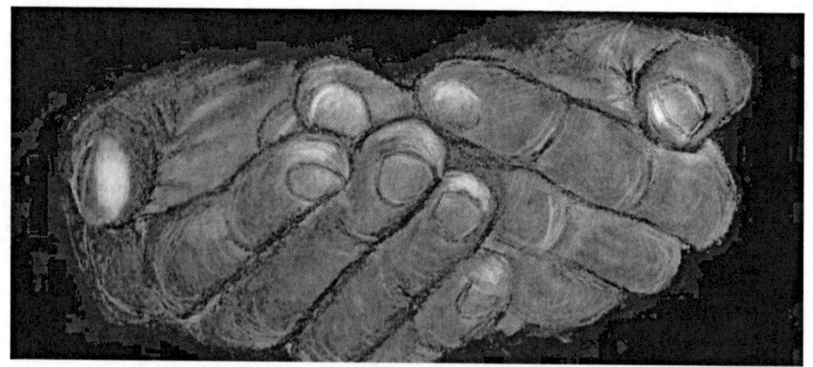

In God's Hands

REV. DR. LARRY A. BROOKINS

When life seems rough, when life gets tough,

When life grows cold and years turn old; put your life in God's Hands.

When friends are few, when money is low,

When death is calling and your tears flow; put your life in God's Hands.

In God's Hands is security. In God's Hands is safety. In God's Hands is protection. In God's Hands is shelter.

In God's Hands is provision. In God's Hands is consolation. In God's Hands is peace. In God's Hands is love.

In God's Hands is mercy. In God's Hands is grace. In God's Hands is forgiveness. In God's Hands is new life.

When questions abound, when answers are unclear,

When decisions are hard and the end of your journey is near;

Put your life in God's Hands. Keep your life in God's Hands.

THERE ARE NO BETTER HANDS TO BE IN THAN **IN GOD'S HANDS**.

Acknowledgments

I want to acknowledge the tremendous contribution of my sister, Charlotte Brookins-Hudson, whose labor of love editing this book has greatly enhanced the message I endeavored to convey. Charlotte's assistance was invaluable to this publication. She helped to improve my sentence structure, punctuation, and thought. Thank you Charlotte for rescuing me and perfecting my flaws. I could not have done it without you! Thank you for your patience and understanding.

Thank you Chiquita George for the concept of our front cover, and thank you Renee K. Robinson for the photo you provided for the back cover. I appreciate you both! Your respective imagery takes us to the cross in reflection and gratitude. Thank you Dr. Dennis J. Woods and Life to Legacy for once again bringing our manuscript to print. Thank you God for the revelation and inspiration. Thank you for your love, sacrifice, and the gift of Your Son Jesus! May this book glorify Thee!

Songs Cited: *No Greater Love* (David L. Allen, 1986), *Jesus Paid It All* (Elvina M. Hall, 1865), *The Old Rugged Cross* (George Bennard, 1912), *Nothing but the Blood* (Robert Lowery, 1876), *There is a Fountain* (William Cowper, 1772), *He Decided to Die* (Donald Vails, 1978), *I Will Trust in the Lord* (Rev. C.L. Franklin, 1978), and *Hold to God's Unchanging Hand* (Jennie B. Wilson, 1906).

Also By Larry A. Brookins

Available for purchase at: www.amazon.com, www.barnesandnoble.com, www.labrookinsministries.org, www.life2legacy.com, and other online retail stores.

About The Author

LARRY A. BROOKINS is Senior Pastor of True Foundation Transformation Church, located in Chicago, IL. He is also the CEO of LA Brookins Ministries, Inc. He is a graduate of Bradley University in Peoria, IL (Bachelor of Fine Arts), Chicago Baptist Institute in Chicago, IL (Associate and Bachelor in Biblical Studies), McCormick Theological Seminary in Chicago, IL (Master of Arts in Theological Studies), and the recipient of Honorary Doctorates from St. Michael's Institute of St. Louis, MO and St. Thomas Christian University of Jacksonville, FL. He is a husband, father, grandfather, as well as a highly proclaimed and sought after preacher and teacher. For more information, visit www.labrookinsministries.org and www.tftchurch.org.

About the Publisher

Let us bring your story to life! With Life to Legacy, we offer the following publishing services: manuscript development, editing, transcription services, ghostwriting, cover design, copyright services, ISBN assignment, worldwide distribution, and eBook production and distribution.

Throughout the entire production process, you maintain control over your project. We also specialize in family history books, so you can leave a written legacy for your children, grandchildren, and others. You put your story in our hands, and we'll bring it to literary life! We have several publishing packages to meet all your publishing needs.

Call us at: 877-267-7477, or you can also send e-mail to: Life2Legacybooks@att.net. Please visit our website: www.Life2Legacy.com

CPSIA information can be obtained
at www.ICGtesting.com
Printed in the USA
FSOW01n1525170516
20461FS